THE
NICK POEMS

WRITTEN BY
ANTHONY BERNAL

LOREA PRESS LOS ANGELES 2011

The Nick Poems Copyright © 2009 by Anthony Bernal

Bernal, Anthony David, 1964-
   The Nick Poems.

Cover Art and Design David Lomeli
Interior Design/Typesetting: Maggie White
Printing and Binding: Amazon.

Orders, inquiries, and correspondence should be addressed to:

AnthonyBernal.blogspot.com
TheNickPoems@facebook.com

ISBN: 978-0-9845919-0-9

TABLE OF CONTENTS

A Tall Glass of Milk   9

Binky   11

Doc Russell   13

Hippity-Hop   15

Nick and Henry   17

Nick and Herman   19

Nick Poem #8   21

Nick Poem #7   23

The Blue Room   26

The Cats   28

The Fifty-Seven-Foot Boat   30

The Filter   32

The Heart   34

The Itch   36

The Liar   38

The Nun   40

The Death Watch   41

THE
NICK POEMS

A Tall Glass of Milk

Nick and I rode together
at the end of the day
we smoked cigarettes
and delivered flowers
in the nice neighborhood

perfect paint jobs
nice gardens
nice cars

he told me a story about
the day he decided not to take orders
from his father anymore

he got mad at his father
for something or other

come out here and fight!
he told him

no son, I'm not going to do that

come out here you coward!

no, son it's not going to be like that

Nick lost his temper anyway
and took a swing at his dad
catching him on the side of the head

when Nick woke up
there was an icepack on his jaw
and he seemed to remember a punch to his face
that knocked the air out of his stomach

come Saturday morning
bright and early
Nick was outside mowing the lawn
like a good son

he had his push broom
and hedge clippers handy

Nick told me
from that day on
whenever his father dreamt of
a pack of Oreo cookies
he dreamt of a tall glass of milk

BINKY

Binky asked Nick
if he'd buy him a gun

Binky couldn't buy a gun
on account he was a convicted felon

Nick respectfully declined

a couple of weeks later
Nick's house was broken into
and two of his guns were stolen

Nick had a feeling
the burglar was Binky

when Nick saw Binky next
he told him that someone
broke into his house
and stole his guns
and that he believed
it was someone he knew
who took them

he told Binky
that it would be okay
for "whoever took the guns"
to give them back to Bink
so Binky could give them back to Nick
and all would be forgiven

Binky didn't take the hint
he never returned the guns

Nick swore someday Binky would get his

months passed
then Nick received a phone call
from the Los Angeles police department

he was informed that one of his guns
was found in a back alley
and that the gun was used in a robbery

Damn that Binky!

Nick hadn't seen Binky for some time
until one day he noticed a familiar
face standing on the corner

Nick honked his horn
and yelled
hey Bink!

Binky turned to notice Nick
waving at him
he waved back

when the light turned green
and Binky stepped away from the curb
Nick noticed that Binky was walking with
a pronounced limp

gunshot wound Nick presumed
a grin came to Nick's face
sweet revenge

Doc Russell

Nick and Doc Russell
were fishing off a bridge
catching spots
when a man approached
to ask how they caught so many fish

what kind of bait are you using
the man asked

shrimp

I'm using shrimp
and I haven't got but a nibble
the man said

what else are you doing? the man asked

Nick and Doc thought they'd have some fun
at the man's expense

well, Doc Russell said
when you catch the first fish
you've got to kiss it
and throw it back in the water
that way the fish will tell his friends
that there's nice people fishing on the bridge

kiss the first fish
the man said as he walked away

the man came back an hour later

I caught ten spots but now I want to
catch a catfish, what do I do to catch a catfish?

Doc Russell pointed to Nick for the answer

well, Nick said, I get the shrimp
and I hold it in my hand
then I put my hand down my pants
and rub my balls with the shrimp
I rub them real good then put the
shrimp on the hook
that's how I catch catfish

I'll try that the man said

an hour or so passed before the man
came back

you fellows sure know how to fish
I've caught five catfish one after another

it wasn't till later
on the way home
that Doc Russell and Nick
started to laugh

they were laughing so hard
they had to pull to the side of the road
to catch their breath

that dumb son of a bitch
he did just as we told him
Doc Russell said

yeah, and he caught some fish too
Nick said

they laughed until
they couldn't laugh anymore
then they drove away
still laughing

HIPPITY-HOP

Hippity-Hop
had a bedroom separate
from the house
upstairs
above the garage

Nick used a ladder
to climb into her window

the next day at school
Hippity-Hop said hello to Nick

but Nick just ignored her

you liked me last night!
I was good enough for you last night!

Nick pretended not to know
what she was talking about
but Nick's friends knew
what she was talking about

lo and behold
Nick found himself
at the free-throw line
of the Florida state basketball championship

his team was down one
with one second left on the clock
it was a two shot foul

he made the first free-throw
and then sank the second

the crowd went berserk
and ran onto the court

they were led by a woman
with a get along in her stride
it was Hippity-Hop

she limped right toward Nick
at full steam
bulled him over
and smothered him with kisses

get her off me
Nick told his good-looking girlfriend

I guess it's true
his girlfriend said before
she walked away

Nick was in the newspaper
the following day
he was front page news

the headline read
State Champions!

below the caption was a black and white picture
of Nick lying on his back
his head was turned to one side
there was an awful look on his face

Hippity-Hop
was on top of him
kissing him with her big ugly lips

NICK AND HENRY

Nick and Henry
went to the hills
to share a bottle

it was late in the day
they were perched on a cliff
enjoying the sunset

a young couple showed up
with a picnic basket and a blanket
and found a spot under a tree

they couldn't see
Nick and Henry
from where they sat

out came the
wine and cheese

Nick and Henry didn't pay
much attention to them
until they started to undress
then they became very interested

the woman was naked
and on her back
the man was on top of her

at first Nick and Henry were happy
to have such a good seat
but after a while when they realized
the man wasn't going about it right
they decided to have some fun

Nick snuck over to a tree
and shook a branch
and Henry made a low
grunting sound like a bear

they were subtle at first
doing just enough to get
the couple's attention

when they had their attention
they stepped it up a bit

what's that?
the woman said

nothing the man answered
he kept at it

the woman was distracted
she was looking around

then Nick shook the tree
and Henry made a grunting sound so ugly
the couple stopped what they were doing
they got up and ran away
and left everything behind
but their clothes

Nick and Henry
waited for them
to come back
but they never did

the men walked toward
the picnic basket
and found the wine

Kendall Jackson

NICK AND HERMAN

When Nick was a teenager
he and his friend Herman
picked up two girls at a JCPenney

they made plans to meet the girls
later that evening
but neglected to tell them
that they had no car
to meet them with

the boys came up with a plan
they were going to wait
until Nick's father fell asleep
at around nine-thirty
then they were going to roll
his car out of the garage
and meet the girls

It was just after nine-thirty
when they snuck into the garage
they put the car in neutral and pushed it

Herman couldn't move the car alone
so Nick got out from behind the wheel to help

they were pushing the car
nice and quiet
when it started to get away from them
the car picked up steam
and rolled down the driveway

Nick hopped into the driver's seat
and tried to steer the car to the street
but when he turned the steering wheel
it locked up on him

he didn't have the sense
to put the key in the ignition

the car smashed into a palm tree
the security lights came on
and Nick's father stood
on the balcony with a shotgun

who's there? he yelled

I got him Dad! Nick shouted

Nick wrestled Herman
to the ground
and held him stiff

I got him!

Nick's dad ran down from the balcony
and pointed the shotgun at Herman's head

Herman?
what are you boys up to?

he tried to steal your car Dad

Herman wouldn't do that.

oh, yes he would.

NICK POEM #8

Nick was driving down Orange Grove Boulevard
when he came upon the Wrigley Mansion

he saw a young woman
in a white summer dress
running across the lawn
there was a man
chasing after her

the man lunged and tackled
the woman to the ground

she was on her back
the man was on top of her
choking and punching her

Nick pulled over
and ran to help the girl

he jumped on the man
and swung his fist at his head

CUT!

WHAT THE HELL ARE YOU DOING ON
MY SET?

Nick looked up and saw
the camera crew for the first time

everybody started to laugh
everybody but the director

my hero, the young lady said

Nick got up and dusted himself off
he was embarrassed
he had a sheepish look on his face

he turned to the young lady
if you need me
I'll be over there
by my car

NICK POEM #7

When Nick was married
he was playing music
for a soul review

Motown
the real Motown

he was faithful to his wife
even though there was
a woman in his bed
after every show
and he was just the bass player

he was making
a lot of money
at the time
he owned a house
had stocks
a nice car
with money in the bank

come to pass
he came home
from tour a day early
and found his wife
in bed with another man

it was bad news
that ended in divorce

a court date was set
to settle the estate

the judge sided with Nick's
wife on most things

he had to give up
the stocks
most of the cash
half of the house
and all the furniture

Nick couldn't believe it

you mean to tell me a man finds his wife
in bed with another man
and he still has to pay her money?

it's the law of the state of California.

you no good mother!
why should I pay her?
she's the adulterer

it's the law of the state of California.

you mother!

sir, one more outburst

this is an outrage!

Nick stormed out of the courtroom
and slammed the door shut
behind him when he left

but the door had a hydraulic hinge on it
and it didn't slam the way it was supposed to
instead it closed painfully slow

Nick looked up
and could hear the air
leaking out of the hinge

he stood and watched
as the door slowly closed

when the door finally shut
it didn't close with a slam
but rather, with a
mechanically engineered click.

THE BLUE ROOM

Nick got a phone call
from a hootchie momma
who wanted to visit him
for old times' sake

the woman took the gold line
into old town Pasadena
where Nick picked her up

she looked good
he hadn't seen her in years
but she still looked good

Nick's plan was to get her drunk
and take her into what he referred
to as the "stabbin-cabin"
or what the boys called
the blue room
a makeshift construction
that sat near the pool

the blue room was lined
with blue plastic
to keep the rain out
any woman who went inside it
had to be crazy

Nick brought the hootchie momma
back to his house

she wanted wine
Nick had the presence of mind
to have bought an Australian brand
for the occasion

she drank the first bottle
and wanted more

Nick had the presence of mind
to have bought two bottles

you don't have to get me drunk
to get some the woman told him

I don't

no you don't

why didn't you
tell me that before
you drank the wine
I could have saved myself
nine dollars and fifty-seven cents

The Cats

Nick was driving down the road
with a car full of kittens
when he was stopped by
a police officer for speeding

I've got to get to the veterinarian
these kittens are very sick
they need attention immediately

Is that why you were speeding?

Yes officer

I'll tell you what
I'll give you a police escort

Thank you officer

the veterinarian was
outside smoking a cigarette
when he saw the flashing lights from
the police car approach

Are you the vet?
the officer asked

Yes I am

This man has some very sick kittens
on his hands they need attention immediately
the officer said before he drove off

I've never seen such a thing
a police escort for sick kittens
the veterinarian said to Nick

yeah, and the funny thing is
those cats aren't sick.

THE FIFTY-SEVEN-FOOT BOAT

Man I'm tired of working,
Nick said to me one morning

didn't your daddy leave
you any money
I asked

Nick's daddy was rich

he turned to me
and made an awful face
full of disgust

all he left me was a fifty-seven-foot boat
do you know how hard it is to sell
a fifty-seven-foot boat?

I hated that boat
I needed three certified sailors
just to operate it
do you know how expensive
three certified sailors can be?

it took me eleven years to sell that boat

had to pay mooring expenses
upkeep
man, I hated that boat

I let my cousin "the chicken man" use it
he'd take it out and let a group
of swingers do their thing

the mayor got wind of it
tried to put a stop to it

but, his son was onboard
so he couldn't say much

the boat just sat after that

until I sold it for next to nothing
to a man I like to refer to as
the luckiest man in the world

THE FILTER

Nick's swimming pool needed
a new pool filter
but he didn't have
the money to buy one

he knew of an abandoned house
that had a pool
his friend had lived there
so he knew all about it

the house was going to be demolished
but Nick had an idea for the filter

he drove over one night
with a hacksaw
and cut one section of pipe here
and another section of pipe there

he lifted the filter up and out
and carried it to his car

he tossed it in the trunk
and boogied

he saw a light turn on
from a neighbor's house
across the street
but he looked straight ahead
he didn't look sideways or backwards
just straight ahead

he found some fittings and adaptors
in his garage
and pieced things together

he flicked the switch
and things turned clean

he had an idea for his old filter
he was going to use it as a
prototype for a pressure cooker

he said he could fit a turkey and ham in it
or four whole chickens
depending on his mood
and culinary desires

THE HEART

Steve Disney greeted
me in the garage
when I got to work

he had a strange look on his face
as he walked toward me

we shook hands

they just took Nick away
in an ambulance
he collapsed and started to convulse
I think he had a heart attack

I found out later
that Nick turned cold
and a deep shade of blue
that his heart had stopped

he was saved by two office girls
who gave him mouth to mouth resuscitation

when he came to he was on a stretcher
and started to yell at the paramedics

who the hell are you?
get your hands off me!
I'm going to knock you out!
I'm fine!
get me off this thing!

I went to the hospital
after work and there he was in bed
looking like nothing happened

Mr. Moffett "the Lovable crook" showed up
he told stories about his pacemaker
he pulled down his shirt to show it off

funny thing about my pacemaker, Moffett said
I got a call from my doctor the other day

you know that pacemaker you have?
the doctor said

yeah, what about it?

it's been recalled
you're going to have to
bring it in for servicing

THE ITCH

When I bet Derrick
I lose

when Nick bets Derrick
he wins

what gives? I asked Nick

my neck was itching

your neck was itching?

when my neck itches I never lose
case in point he told me

last week my neck was itching
so I bought a daily three ticket
and won $467
I have the cash to prove it

one day a long time ago
my neck was itching

I drove to Santa Anita racetrack
then straight to Alston Ford from there
and bought myself a brand new
1972 Ford Galaxy with a landau top
with the winnings

another time I needed $17,000
for a down payment for a house
my neck started to itch

I drove to Los Alamitos racetrack
but it was closed

so I drove to Del Mar
and came back with $15,000

it doesn't itch often
but when it does
it's guaranteed

THE LIAR

Nick had a girl that he'd
see from time to time
it was nothing serious
she was just someone
to fill the space of need

he went to see her one day
and she told him that
she was pregnant

Nick looked at her with a grin
it's my child?

it's your child she told him

Nick chuckled

then he explained to her
the impossibility of it all
on account of him being snipped

you must be a sorry woman
to pick me to be the father
if I'm the best man
out of all the men you're seeing
that's sorry in itself

she tried to deny
that she was seeing other men
which only made Nick mad

he finally lost his temper
when he couldn't take
the lying anymore

he beat her real bad
blood everywhere
he nearly killed her

THE NUN

Dad

I hit a nun today

you did what?

I hit a nun

why?

because every time I hit
a wrong note on the piano
she'd whap me on my fingers with her ruler
I told her to stop
but she wouldn't listen
so I hit her
I hit her so hard
she fell off her stool

are you nuts?
son, don't you know
that's like hitting god himself
you might as well have punched Jesus

Baby, did you hear what your son did today?
he whapped a nun so hard
she fell off the piano stool
your boy has lost his mind
he has simply LOST his mind.

THE DEATH WATCH

Nick had a cold he couldn't shake
he checked himself into the hospital
and was diagnosed with pneumonia

I paid him a visit
he seemed okay

he had an oxygen mask
in his hand
it was hooked up to a machine
that beeped when he was talking too much
and not breathing with the mask enough

a couple of weeks later
the doctors collapsed his lungs
to take a culture to try to figure out
what strain of pneumonia he had

he was never the same after that

he went from talking
and having a good time
to being drugged and asleep

with the drugs came tubes and wires
and an assortment of strange devices

there was something that
looked like a car radiator
on the floor
there were fluids everywhere
a breathing tube in his mouth

he just lay there after that

I paid him a visit after work
it was just he and I
he lay there weak
the best he could do
was squeeze my hand

I saw him two or three times more
before I got a call from Mickey

he has two days to live, Mickey said

two days to live
for what started off as a cold

I showed up both days
his lungs were shot
he couldn't breathe on his own

he was hooked up to a machine
and his chest jerked with each breath

he had no strength
it was a miracle when he
opened his eyes

but he opened his eyes for me
he looked right at me
when I walked into the room
and smiled at me with his eyes

his eyes were cloudy
glossy
weak
but he smiled

I held his gaze
the best I could
I smiled back

I felt foolish smiling at a dying man
my eyes turned away
and he closed his

the death watch ended
a day and a morning later

www.ingramcontent.com/pod-product-compliance
Lightning Source LLC
Chambersburg PA
CBHW060633030426
42337CB00018B/3347